WHO IS THE HONORABLE
MINISTER LOUIS FARRAKHAN

By Rasheed L. Muhammad

Co Author Abdul Wahid Muhammad

Copyright 2021

Contents

"And [remember] when Moses prayed for water for his people and We replied, "Strike the rock with thy staff!"- whereupon twelve springs gushed forth from it, so that all the people knew whence to drink. [And Moses said:] "Eat and drink the sustenance provided by God, and do not act wickedly on earth by spreading corruption." Holy Quran 2:60

Preface

I have been a registered member of the Nation of Islam for nearly 60 years. My early years were under the leadership of the Most Honorable Elijah Muhammad, my role was building up membership throughout the western region of the United States. I served as Lieutenant and public relations for the Nation. I saw Elijah Muhammad's teachings reform people right before my eyes. The downtrodden, prostitutes, criminals and drug addicts. People would hear the teachings and would go off in their eyes.

During those years, I also had a personal relationship and friendship with Minister Louis Farrakhan before he became the National Representative of the Honorable Elijah Muhammad in 1965.

In 1977 I was the first follower of Minister Louis Farrakhan after he began to rebuild the Nation of Islam from its fall, to which this book shall address. Under his leadership I once served as assistant Supreme Captain, National Secretary and Business Manager of the Nation. I currently function as a National Consultant. What I see him doing do is the same work done by the Honorable Elijah Muhammad. Through the mouth of the Minister, the thugs, gang members, downtrodden, prostitutes, criminals, and drug addicts were cleaned up and reformed. Both these men's mission is on a scale of biblical proportion, to which this book shall address.

I worked diligently under Elijah Muhammad's leadership as I have under Minister Farrakhan because I also see him fulfilling a divine role mentioned in both Bible and Quran, to which this book shall address.

This book is like a documentary or *"bookcumentary"* about the birth, life and mission of the Honorable Minister Louis Farrakhan. It is replete with pictures of his childhood, his mother, friends, well-wishers, and international travels. What you shall read about is his childhood background, high school and college years. His success as a professional musician, and violinist. Midcourse in the book, you read when he first met Malcolm X and the Honorable Elijah Muhammad, and why the Nation of Islam fell in 1975.

Toward the closing of this book, clarity is written about how, and why Minister Farrakhan came to rebuild the Nation of Islam in 1977, who was sent to retrieve him and why a segment of the Jewish community hate him for speaking the gospel truth going on 66 years (1955 to 2021), to which this book gives importance found in the subtitle of this book, *Quran and Return Of Jesus.*

The most profound aspect to this little book, *"Who Is The Honorable Minister Louis Farrakhan"* is its summary that demonstrates a theological, and mathematical congruency that Jesus is and has been in our mist. But you have to read the book to comprehend it.

Abdul Wahid Muhammad

3/26/2021

Chapter 1

What's In A Name 1933

The Honorable Minister Louis Farrakhan was born Louis Eugene Walcott on May 11, 1933, in The Bronx, New York City. (See photo below) Sarah Mae Manning, and Percival Clark were his parents. His mother was born in Saint Kitts, while his father was Jamaican, whom the Minister has never known except to say that his father was a very light skin man.

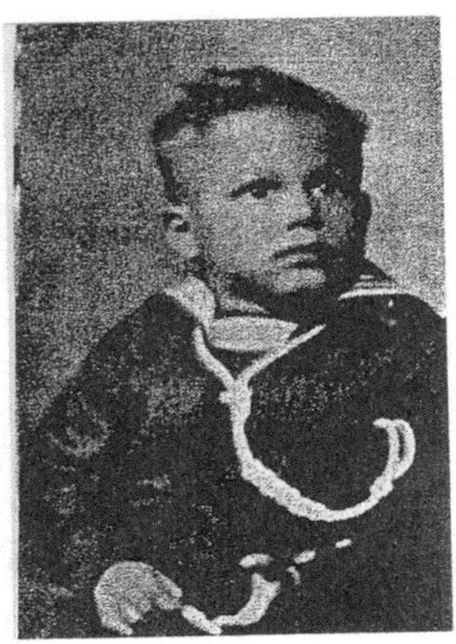

Sarah Mae Manning

The names of mother's origin and history Sarah means "my princess", and Mae means bitter or pearl; also it is a nickname used for Mary. On the hand his father's name Clark means "scribe", secretary" or a scholar within a religious order referring to someone who was educated". Last in order of mention is their child given the name; Eugene. An English form of Eugenius, the Latin form of the Greek, Eugenios which derive from the Greek word "eugenes" meaning "well born" of a noble family.

Chapter 2

Well Born Child 1938

As a very little boy, young Louis, his mother, and older brother moved to Boston, Massachusetts in Lower Roxbury area. It was here wherein he was surrounded by a great influence of his West Indian community. During these formative years, a strong sense of family, education, church, and music won the day. His mother gave him his first violin in 1938, at age 5. She also engaged her sons in what we now call "black talk" and exposed them with "Black" consciousness reading materials such as The Crisis Magazine published by the NAACP.

In the picture above you see to your far right, Alvan Walcott, older brother of young Louis. This photo was taken in front the church they attended, St. Cyprian's Episcopal Church. It was at this church wherein young Louis Gene Walcott began to seek answers to questions that no one seemed to be willing to answer. Questions concerning the state of black people in general, and God's omnipresence yet blacks were in crisis. In recounting his early life, the Honorable Minister Louis Farrakhan stated during an interview concerning these matters:

"I always felt the pain of those that I would read about in *The Crisis Magazine*, or in *The Afro-American* or *The Pittsburgh Courier*, when we would read of the lynching's and the burnings and the castrations and the terrible torture of Black people when White people felt that we had done something improper," Minister Farrakhan said in Part 7 of his lecture series, *The Time and What Must be Done*. "And so my heart

ached to see our people free; so, I started to look for

somebody who would address the concerns of our people..."[1]

In 1944, young Louis, age 11, was visiting his uncle for the summertime. He noticed on the wall a picture of a black man

unlike the pictures at his mother's home placed on the mantelpiece Queen Elizabeth, King George and a white representation of Jesus. However, he asked his uncle who was the black man. His uncle told him that was Marcus Garvey 'who came to unite Black people'.

It was during the summer of 1944 that Louis Gene Walcott was told by his uncle that his father was a follower of Marcus Garvey and that his mother was on the fringe of the Garvey Movement. The young persistent nephew than asked his uncle: "Where is he that I might go and be with him?' and my uncle said, 'He's passed away.'" Minister Farrakhan recounted. "And the

---

[1] A Leader From Birth: A Look Into Ministers Farrakhan's Early Life By JoshuasTruth.com, May 2, 2018

tears fell from my eyes, because I had come that close to what my heart was yearning for, and he was gone."[2]

Uncle of Minister Farrakhan, Brother Samuel Farrakhan

Along with his families black conscious leanings, playing the violin most certainly was a part of the Ministers early childhood development. Science finds that the brain is actually modified physically by studying the violin in ways that make it easier to learn more. The cerebral cortex, the site of higher thinking in the brain, is not a static structure. Its organization changes over time, giving the brain an astonishing ability to adapt to new needs.[3]

To make my point, in 1946 Eugene Louis Walcott, age 13, appeared on the Ted Mack Original Amateur Hour to play his violin and he won an award.[4]

Another famous performer to appear and win on that show was Gladys Knight, in 1952.

---

[2] A Leader From Birth: A Look Into Ministers Farrakhan's Early Life By JoshuasTruth.com, May 2, 2018

[3] www.violinist.com/blog/paulinefiddle/200610/5901/

[4] See Youtube: Minister Louis Farrakhan 1949

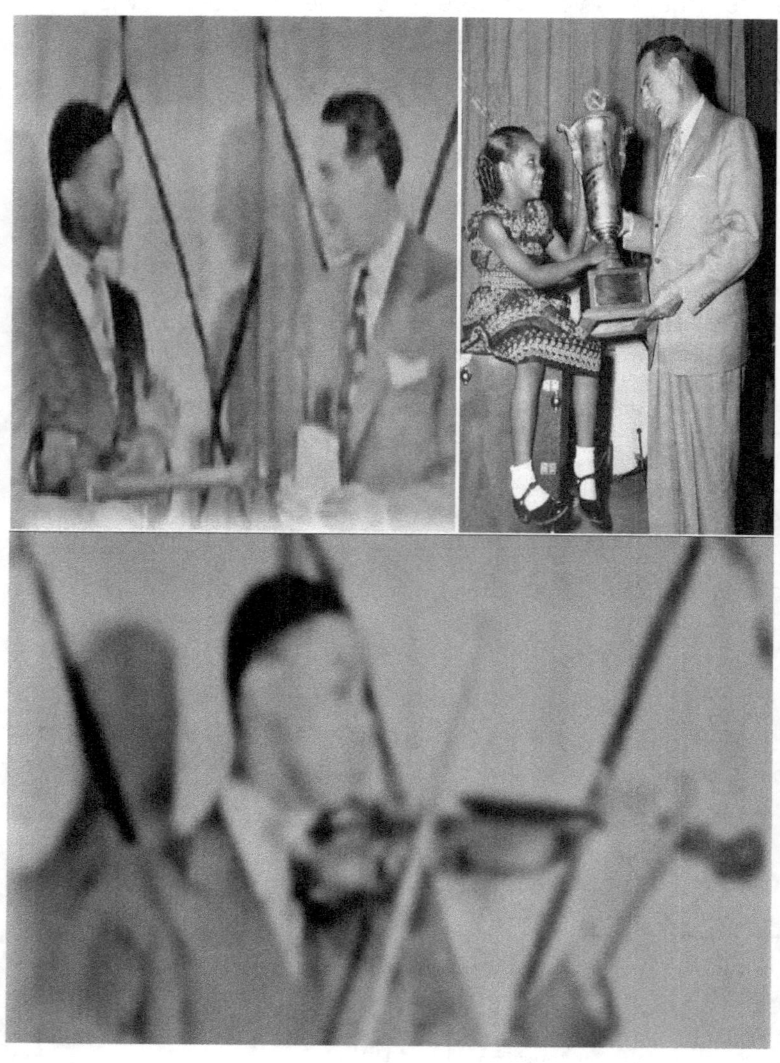

Chapter 3

Three Years Of College

After the Minister graduated at age 16 from English High of Boston with a background in Latin. Not only did he play classical violin, he was also a track star. Subsequently, he received a track scholarship to attend Winston-Salem Teachers College. Then, during his college sophomore year, on February

EUGENE WALCOTT   HORACE HEIDT

Eugene Walcott, 19, sophomore at Winston-Salem Teachers College, was selected to play his violin on the Horace Heidt show, "The American Way," on Thursday, February 26, 1953. Walcott had previously won a first place prize of $50 on Saturday, February 21, 1953.

Horace Heidt called Walcott back-stage after the show and offered him the chance to appear on the nationwide network. Heidt referred to Walcott as "a great artist."

Here's to success, Gene!!

26, 1953, he was selected to play his violin on a famous television program, at age 20, on The Horace Heidt Show.

As fate would have it, the **well born child** did not complete his college 4-year term. He only completed three years. His longtime sweetheart, Betsy Ross (now known as Mother Khadijah Farrakhan), became pregnant with their first child. So he decided to leave college, get married and take care of his family by going into show business.

Chapter 4

On The Road To Fame 1953

The Ministers famous genre of entertainment was Calypso. This form of music can be traced back to West African Kaiso and the arrival of French planters and their slaves from the French Antilles in the 18th century. It is characterized by highly rhythmic and harmonic vocals, and is most often sung in a French creole and led by a griot.[5]

After beginning his professional career, he was known as "The Charmer" performing in nightclubs covering the northeastern and Midwestern territories. His nickname on the street was "Calypso Gene" This well born child was on the road to stardom as an entertainer. In 1953 he was producing records and once referred to as 'Trinidad's Newest Sensation'.

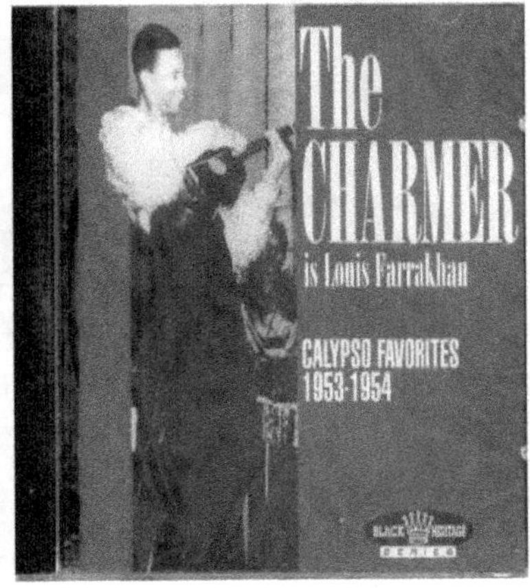

---

[5] *Atilla's **Kaiso**: a short history of Trinidad calypso* (1983).

Among those whom frequented night clubs and the streets, they heard about the "Charmer". His songs from 1953 to 1954 lists as follows:

1. IS SHE IS, OR IS SHE AIN'T

2. BROWN SKIN GAL

3. DON'T TOUCH ME NYLON

4. ZOMBIE JAMBOREE

5. FEMALE BOXER

6. FIRE DOWN THERE

7. UGLY WOMAN

8. DON'T LET ME MAMA KNOW

9. STONE COLD MAN

10. MARY ANN

11. HOLD 'EM JOE

12. TRINIDAD ROAD MARCH

As a young handsome rising entertainer, Louis Eugene Walcott came to earn $500 per week touring. By todays standard that is $5,519 per week if adjusted for inflation. Again, $500 in 1954 is equal to $5,519 in 2021. Annual inflation over this period was 3.44%. Value of a dollar.[6]

---

[6] www.in2013dollars.com/us/inflation/1950?amount=500

In spite of all his success, deep in his soul, he yet yearned for something greater in terms of freedom, justice and equality for the suffering black people of America.

Chapter 5

Elijah Prays For A Helper 1954

By the time year 1954 commenced, the Nation of Islam had been established in North America, under that leadership of the Honorable Elijah Muhammad for 24 years. His pioneer ministers had worked with him with the best of their abilities. His newest and youngest minister during the 1954 Saviors Day Convention was Malcom X who had registered in 1952. Yet, Elijah prayed for a special helper.[7]

(first row L-R) Minister Isaiah Karriem, Bro. Clarence, Bro. Elmer, Minister Sultan Muhammad, Minister James Shabazz, Minister Benjamin Muhammad and Bro. Jake. (second row) Bro. Charles X Worthington, Bro. Richard, Bro. John, Bro. Herbert, and other NOI Pioneers of Washington, D.C.

---

[7] <u>Saviour's day 1954 - YouTube</u>, Part 1 & Part 2.

Min. Lucius Bey (at podium), seated from L-R Min. Asbury X, Min. George X, Min. Isaiah Karriem, Min. R.T. X, Min. Malcolm X and Min. Ulysses X

As stated earlier, Saviors Day 1954, the Honorable Elijah Muhammad publically said he desired a little helper and I quote: "...we have been so gravely misunderstood, that I desire that Allah send to me a little helper. For 22 years, I have worked hard where ever I was or maybe, to try to get into your ears and into your hearts the truth that Allah has revealed to me."[8] These words imply that Mr. Muhammad realized his message needed to be presented by a helper whom would come at a future date to make it his teachings better understood from the way it was presented by his faithful pioneers.

---

[8] Saviors Day 1954 Part 1 (youtube) 8:16 seconds into lecture

Among those early pioneer ministers of the Honorable Elijah Muhammad (H.E.M) is Lucius X standing on the rostrum (see pg. 16). Minister Lucius X became a registered member of the Nation of Islam in 1939. He became known as Minister Lucius Bey Muhammad, the Dean of Ministers of the Honorable Elijah Muhammad. He was taught by H.E.M. for 3 ½ years while living in his home.

At another point in time, 1965, the next minister whom would live in the home of H.E.M. to be taught directly by H.E.M. for several years, was Minister Barnard Cushmeer. Ironically, he was born in the same hospital as Minister Farrakhan except 3 years later. As a young man, he played drums. More on that history.

Just as today, famous entertainers always attract attention, so it was during the 1930's, 40's and 50's. And so, one such famous entertainer to get to Mr. Muhammad was named "The Charmer". He was called thusly owing to the way he sang his songs and his charming personality. Moreover, he was one of the most famous Calypso singers during that era. Is that one reason Malcolm X went to see and hear "The Charmer" in 1952 perform at Eddie Levine's nightclub in Boston. Little did Malcolm X know that the young man would one day use his stringed instrument and voice in the worship of God?

Chapter 6

Louis X 1955

Before Elijah Muhammad's words were fulfilled regarding his little helper, Eugene Louis Walcott was told a few years earlier, by a friend, that a messenger of God was among Black people. He recounts:

"I When Farrakhan was 19, he had heard from a friend that "God had chosen a messenger for us." Although a messenger is exactly what Minister Farrakhan was looking for, this news hurt him.

"As I walked the street, tears fell from my eyes, and I asked God: 'God, why didn't you choose me? You know I love my people...' And as fast as I made that question to God, the answer came when the brother had told me that 'God appeared in 1930' and I was not even born. So I decided I

must go and meet this man, and offer him my life," *Farrakhan said.*[9]

The question becomes: what were you thinking at age 19? In any case, the F.O.I. did not know what the "Charmer" was thinking as he toured performing his music. I mean, regardless of his success in school, track and music, his mind had been suggesting to him that he was to do something for his people to help them get out of oppression and tyranny. But what he had to fulfill in his life had not yet materialized.

In 1952, Malcolm X came to hear and see "The Charmer" while playing at a nightclub in Boston called Eddie Levine's nightclub across from Wally's Paradise. He first saw him after coming out in-between a set to quickly greet and shake Malcolm's hand. Of course, the he had heard about Malcolm X prior to that brief encounter, but was not too much interested in what Malcolm X was known to teach regarding "white folks".[10] Then three years later, the stage was set to seal "The Charmer". In 1955 when he came to Chicago to perform at a club called the *Blue Angel,* his heart and mind was sealed to fulfill what his soul desired from an early age. That was to help his people in the liberation struggle toward freedom, justice and equality.

At some point during his time in Chicago, Eugene Louis Walcott was invited by one of his friends to hear the Honorable Elijah Muhammad speak during the Nation of Islam's Saviors Day

---

[9] A Leader From Birth: A Look Into Ministers Farrakhan's Early Life By JoshuasTruth.com, May 2, 2018

[10] Louis Farrakhan speaks on Malcolm X (1979) Pt.1 (Listen 1:00:10 sec. into lecture)

Convention. And for friendships sake, he decided to attend along with his wife and his first daughter, Betsy Gene, in spite of hearing people say Elijah Muhammad was a hate teacher and radical. What he did not know; of course, was that Mr. Muhammad was told about this young man's presence in town.

"...Minster Malcolm X was informed that the popular musician would attend the convention. An arrangement was made between the Honorable Elijah Muhammad, Minister Malcolm and his Captain, Yusef Shah, that latter was to sit next to young Louis in such a way that the Honorable Elijah Muhammad might recognize him,..[11]

Muhammad's Temple No. 2, at 5333 South Woodlawn Chicago, Il.

---

[11] Saviours' Day 2002 Special Edition

The picture is the location where the well born child first heard the Most Honorable Elijah Muhammad speak in 1955. As you have read, Elijah Muhammad instructed a particular F.O.I. captain to sit next to the special visitor. He was placed in the balcony in order that he and others could get a direct view of him to see his response to the teachings.

Being proficient in the English language, the Minister thought himself, as the Honorable Elijah Muhammad began to teach, he thought to himself, 'This man can't speak', This was due to H.E.M. splitting verbs during his lecture. As soon as the Minister thought these thoughts, he said the Honorable Elijah Muhammad looked directly up at him and said, "Brother, I did not have a chance to get that mighty fine education that you received, when I got to the school, the door was closing. Don't you pay no attention to how I'm saying it, you pay attention to what I'm saying. Then you take it and put it in that fine that you know. Only try to understand what I'm saying."[12]

Naturally, the Minister was shocked because he felt the Honorable Elijah Muhammad was reading his mind. Then he shrunk back in his seat. Nevertheless, right after the lecture, the Minister and his wife accepted to teachings on that day of February 26, 1955.[13] One of his first major test came within 3 months. Minister Malcolm X announced that all registered Muslims had to get out of the show business or get out of the

---

[12] Saviours' Day 2002 Special Edition
[13] (See Youtube: How Elijah of Your Bible Met Minister Farrakhan

Temple. Well, Brother Louis X chose to leave show business to dedicate his life to the teachings of the Honorable Elijah Muhammad.

Chapter 7

Muhammad's Temple No. 11

Eugene Louis Walcott was now known as Brother Louis X and one day during a men's training class, he was allowed to speak to the F.O.I., wherein he enthusiastically pronounced that he would 'take the teachings of the Honorable Elijah Muhammad to every nook and cranny around the world!' At this early beginning of his service; of course, he had no idea about the three world tours he'd undergo 40 years later.

After moving to Boston, very early on, Brother Louis X was made captain over the F.O.I. and by 1956, he was made minister over Muhammad's Temple No. 11. The good fortune about his early development as an F.O.I. was that Malcolm X was his mentor whom he tried to follow in demeanor out of love and admiration.

The picture says it all. The young Minister, Louis X was being groomed by soldiers of the Honorable Elijah Muhammad.

Attempt To Kill Minister Louis X In Boston

As a newly dedicated Minister of Temple No. 11, Minister Louis X lived the Restrictive Laws of the Nation of Islam to the hilt! And when a believer broke the law, he put them out of the Temple for a prescribed time, according the laws governing the Temple. Well young Minister Louis X was so hard on law breakers that he had 40 believers out. Not knowing his great future, this too would become another great lesson for his future work. So lets us read the story, in his words, about what happened:

"I was a young Minister at time, and I made some mistakes, honest to God. They were moral. I clinged to the law but I was ignorant and I mishandled authority and I drove 40 people out the Temple in Boston....that's a whole Temple.

They were writing to the Messenger (Elijah Muhammad) complaining on this terrible minister...The Messenger sent for me...He looked at his little foolish minister and he said that I was sincere but my mistakes were made through ignorance. He didn't tell me not to go back and do my job, He told me to go on back to my post...Then the Messenger said, 'I think this brother will do

MUHAMMAD'S TEMPLE NO. 11
35 INTERVALE STREET   DORCHESTER, MASSACHUSETTS

MINISTER LOUIS X.
A devoted follower of the Honorable Elijah Muhammad

alright. He'll lose 40 today, but he'll get 400,000 for me tomorrow or 400,000,000 for me the day after".[14]

One of the most tragic events to happen to Minister Louis X in Boston occurred when someone or a group of people or government agents attempted to kill him by setting his residence ablaze. He recounts how one night, he, his wife and children were awakened fleeing their burning residence that was set ablaze. In those days, since the ministers of the Temple kept charity in their homes, he decided to go back into the burning place, after all his family had evacuated. Realizing the charity donations were left behind, notwithstanding his own safety, he ran back into the flames to retrieve the believers' charity, thus, giving no reason to later explain *'what happen to the money.'* Here was a great sign of his integrity, courage and character.

---

[14] Youtube 40:15 sec: Minister Farrakhan LA 1979

Through that controversy, Don X Straughter accepted Islam after hearing Minister Louis X teach a 5 hour subject entitled, "Who is God, what is he and where is he". Currently, now known as Minister Don Muhammad, he continues to head up the Boston Mosque No. 11, under his friend and brothers leadership, Minister Farrakhan.

On the on next page is a brief history about Minister Don Muhammad and why he accepted Islam in 1957.

Minister Don Muhammad: Biography

Minister Don Muhammad, a native of Fayetteville, West Virginia, originally traveled to Boston as a teenager in the early 1950s during summer school vacations to visit his older brother and to savor the Boston experience. Upon graduation he made Boston his permanent residence. Always recognized as an industrious and studious individual then Don Straughter, who had played semi-pro baseball and had an undying love for football, became an entrepreneur, establishing his own cleaners business at a very young age.

Building a business and family would have seemed to be a handful for this young man and his wife, Sister Shirley; now married for 48 years. Though in 1957, he heard the word of The Honorable Elijah Muhammad delivered by a young minister named Louis X, and later had the opportunity to hear directly from The Honorable Elijah Muhammad during one of his visits to Boston, Bro. Don accepted Islam as taught by The Honorable Elijah Muhammad and committed himself to the elevation of self, family, and community. Bro. Don worked closely with the young Minister Louis X, now known as The Honorable Minister Louis Farrakhan; Minister Malcom X; and was blessed to have received direct personal instructions from The Most Honorable Elijah Muhammad.

Bro. Don assisted in the establishment of the then Muhammad's Temple No. 11, which was located on Intervale Street in Dorchester. With steadfast commitment and perseverance he served in many capacities, which included but were not limited to salesman, truck driver, teacher, administrator, lieutenant, captain, minister, and all-round taskmaster. He had the uncanny ability to balance his duties with his other obligations of building his business and family, which includes five children and ten grandchildren.

Chapter 8

Who Is Farrakhan 1965

After Malcolm X was assassinated in 1965, by some United States Federal Agents, three months later, the Honorable Elijah Muhammad relocated Minister Louis X from Boston to New York to minister over Harlem's Temple No. 7. He also assigned the 32 year old minister with a new holy name, FARRAKHAN, and made him his National Representative!

Local U.S. government officials took advantage of the anger and confusion behind Malcolm's murder and rumored Nation of Islam member involvement.

However, at that moment in time, the name Minister Louis X was not even remotely associated with the death of Malcolm X. Such propaganda began 30 or so years later.

At any rate, by the powers that be, the New York Harlem Temple was blown up or burnt down, 1965. It was not the work of a "run in the mill crack pot outfit." The fire was a rogue government operation to create a war between and amongst the righteous.

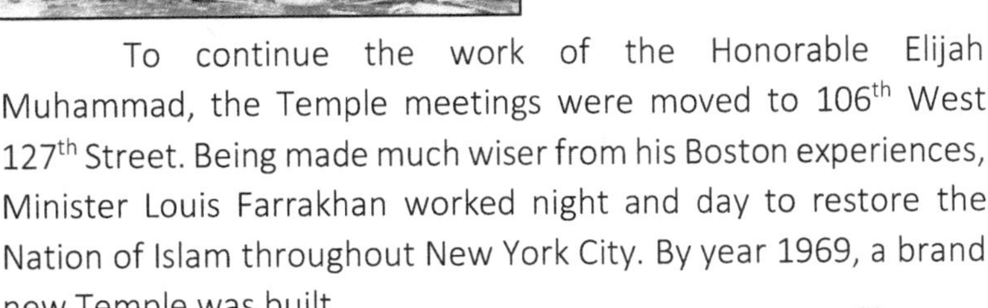

To continue the work of the Honorable Elijah Muhammad, the Temple meetings were moved to 106th West 127th Street. Being made much wiser from his Boston experiences, Minister Louis Farrakhan worked night and day to restore the Nation of Islam throughout New York City. By year 1969, a brand new Temple was built.

Assassination Attempt On Farrakhan 1972

By now it was clear to city officials that the Nation of Islam was reestablished in Harlem and Minister Louis Farrakhan's voice and love was a major key. So on April 14, 1972, as the story goes, an officer called for assistance claiming to be a detective. His call supposedly came from within the Temple where The Minister was working.

"When they arrived, they heard scuffling on the floor above. As they made their way to a staircase they were intercepted by fifteen to twenty men who forced the officers to retreat down the stairs and back into the hallway. Officers Victor Padilla and Ivan Negron, of the 25th Precinct, arrived and entered the premises. The four officers were outnumbered and were then attacked. Navarra was able to escape as a steel door was closed, trapping Cardillo, Padilla and Negron...

"According to the NYPD, the officers were attacked by around fifteen to twenty congregants, were beaten, and stripped of their guns. Padilla was then beaten and <u>*blackjacked*</u> *into semi-consciousness while his partner fought off several men who were trying to grab his* <u>*revolver*</u>*. With his back to the door, Negron suddenly heard shots. He turned and saw a man with a gun in his hand who seemed to be getting up from the floor where Cardillo now lay shot...*

"Cardillo had been assaulted, stripped of his firearm and was shot at point-blank range. Negron, managing to free himself from his attackers, drew his revolver and fired three shots. It is not known if the man with the gun was hit; he escaped. Officer Rudy Andre of

the 28th Precinct broke the glass on the front metal door and saw the patrolmen inside on their backs. He fired several shots through the broken glass into the hallway which scattered the men who had been assaulting the officers, thus enabling Negron to unbolt the double metal door. During the melee, Cardillo and Padilla were seriously injured."[15]

First things first. The lie told about a phone call made from an officer inside the Temple, in distress is counter intelligences modus operandi. They knew Minister Louis Farrakhan was inside the Temple. This rogue operation had planned to do to Minister Farrakhan what it had done to Malcolm X! But they failed. The picture says it all. This scene shows the police officers being dragged away, exhausted, injured and dozy. Some members of the crowd were shouding, "got out of Harlem you devils."

---

[15] The Untold Story Behind the Harlem Mosque Shooting", by Robert Daley. *New York Magazine*. June 4, 1973.

Pictured above is a scene of how many black people in New York City descended upon the Temple. Surrounding the police and to help defend the Muslims, you see thousands. They appeared after word on the street spread that the police attacked the Muslims at Temple No. 7, 125th street.

Pictured below is Minister Louis Farrakhan addressing the crowd after the melee.

"In 1972, when I was minister in New York City, Temple No. 7, the police attacked our mosque. **Within a few hours, Aretha Franklin came to the mosque, to my office, and said that she saw the news and came as quickly as she could to stand with us and offer us her support.** She asked me if Rev. Jesse Jackson had been there to show support. I said, not yet. She said, he'll be here within 48 hours. Rev. Jackson came and stood with the Muslims. We marveled at her show of courage, fearlessness which was rooted in her profound love for her people and her desire for justice for "

The Honorable Minister Louis Farrakhan
Excerpt from official statement on the passing of Aretha Franklin

Temple No. 7, Harlem New York had grown so strong and enduring an d news worthy.

"New York included one of the more than 20 Muhammad University of Islam schools established by the Muslims in the 5 boroughs of New York. Muhammad Temple No. 7 Building, at street level, included a restaurant, bakery, and convenience store. You could find Steak n Take restaurants and Shabazz Bakeries all over New York. Under Minister Farrakhan's leadership, Temple No. 7 imported millions of pounds of whiting fish from Peru and "fed the multitudes" in New York. The number of Muslim followers of The Most Honorable Elijah Muhammad grew far beyond the levels accomplished while Malcolm X was the New York minister."[16]

Chapter 9

Elijah Muhammad Anoints Farrakhan 1972

On July 30, 1972, Minister Farrakhan came to Chicago to hear Mr. Muhammad speak. He sat behind all the other ministers on stage to hear the teacher, teach.

This was during the Theology of Time lecture series, delivered by the Honorable Elijah Muhammad. Remarkably, he instructs his audience to listen to one of his strongest preachers, Minister Farrakhan. He said:

---

[16] http://noirg.org/articles/how-the-bombing-of-temple-no-7-relates-to-the-911-false-. flag-operation/

"I want you to remember today that I have one of my greatest teachers here "... what are you hiding around the sycamore tree for, brother? Come on out here so they can see you. We have with us today our Great National Preacher, the preacher who don't mind going into Harlem, New York, one of the most worst towns in our nation or cities."

"It is our Brother in Detroit or Chicago, or New York. But I want you to remember every week, he is on the air helping me to reach my people that I can't get out of my house to reach like he. I want you to pay good attention to his preaching, his preaching is a bearing of witness to me and what God has revealed to me."

"This is one of the strongest national preachers I have in the bounds of North America. Everywhere you hear him, listen to him; everywhere you see him, look at him; everywhere he advises you to go, go; everywhere he advises you to stay from, stay from; so we are thankful to Allah for his great helper of mine, Minister Farrakhan." [17]

Abdul Akbar Muhammad

Brother Akbar Muhammad, formerly known as Larry X was a very special brother, aid, and assistant to Minister

---

[17] YouTube "Theology of Time 7-30-72: Honorable Elijah Muhammad Anoints Farrakhan").

Farrakhan during the successful restoration of the Harlem Temple during the 1960's.

"New York could not have never been as great as New York was, except I had a friend in Brother Akbar....

"Akbar was always trying to help me do things to bring about a vision that I had but he knew how to make it happen....said Minister Farrakhan"[18]

Black Family Day was an event that frightened New City officials. What was meant by the expression "capture," New York that frightened New York's political leadership? Was it the idea

(L) Larry X looking at Minister Louis Farrakhan viewing crowd of 70,000 at Black Family Day, 1974.

---

[18] Final Call Newspaper, Nov, 12, 2019: A Tribute to Akbar Muhammad

of Black Unity under the leadership of the Hon. Elijah Muhammad?

Akbar Muhammad was one the key people, of many, to help make Black Family Day an overwhelmingly successful event. In fact, Randall's Island was so jam-packed with Black people, Minister Farrakhan had to be flown in by helicopter due to massive traffic jams.

As stated earlier, one vital man behind the success of Black Family Day was Brother Larry X (*Abdul Akbar Muhammad*). The lecture delivered on that day by Minister Louis Farrakhan was also produced into an album for all future generations to hear.

Brother Akbar was actually the person who designed the Album, and produced it with the help of Kenny Gamble[19]

---

[19] Kenny Gamble is a legend in Philadelphia music. One of the most influential soul artists in history, Kenny Gamble helped mold The Sound of Philadelphia.

Currently, Brother Akbar is the international representative of the Honorable Minister Louis Farrakhan. He has traveled to 128 countries on behalf of the Nation of Islam in the West.

During the height of Nations progress and success around the planet, the elder Muslims of the Nation of Islam wondered why the Honorable Elijah Muhammad would say, *"one day the Nation will fall....but it will be rebuilt to never fall again."*

Chapter 10

FBI's Plot On February 25, 1975

Months leading up to the year 1975, the Honorable Elijah Muhammad was in Mexico convalescing. At some point he had entered into a hospital.

However; strange, orders or instructions were sent to the hospital in Mexico to send him (Elijah Muhammad) back to North America. He was then taken to Mercy Hospital in Chicago, Illinois on January 30, 1975.

The question becomes: what role did the FBI have in returning him back to North America, on a 4 hour 20 minute—1,690 mile flight? I pose this question because based on the 1969 FBI file on Elijah Muhammad, the FBI dictated the following:

Counterintelligence Program (FBI File Date: 01-07-1969)

SAC, Chicago (157-2209) January 7, 1969
Director, FBI (100-448006)
COUNTERINTELLIGENCE PROGRAM
BLACK NATIONALIST - HATE GROUPS
RACIAL INTELLIGENCE
(NATION OF ISLAM)

"Although the Nation of Islam (NOI) does not presently advocate violence by its members, the group does preach hatred of the white race and racial separatism. The membership of the NOI is organized and poses a real racial threat. The NOI is responsible for the largest Black Nationalist newspaper, which has been used by other black extremists.

"The NOI appears to be the personal fiefdom of Elijah Muhammad. When he dies a power struggle can be expected and the NOI could change direction. We should be prepared for this eventuality. We should plan how to change the philosophy of the NOI to one of the strictly religious and self-improvement orientation, deleting the race hatred and separate nationhood aspects.

"In this connection Chicago should consider what counterintelligence action might be needed now or at the time of Elijah Muhammad's death to bring about such a change in NOI philosophy. Important considerations should include the identity, strengths, and weaknesses, of any contenders for NOI leadership. What are the positions of our [BUREAU DELETION] informants in regard to leadership? How could potential leaders be turned or neutralized?

"The alternative to changing the philosophy of the NOI is the destruction of the organization. This might be accomplished through generating factionalism among the contenders for Elijah Muhammad's leadership or through legal action in probate court on his death. Chicago should consider the question of how to generate the factionalism necessary to destroy the NOI by splitting into several groups. [BUREAU DELETION]" IJD: ekw

From the above FBI report, the United States Governments top law enforcement agency had written about plans to destroy the Nation of Islam as taught by the Honorable Elijah Muhammad. The report was filed 6 years before it was announce that he died on February 25, 1975 in Mercy Hospital, Chicago Illinois.

On THIS Day

February 26, 1975
OBITUARY

Elijah Muhammad Dead; Black Muslim Leader, 77

Special to THE NEW YORK TIMES

"Chicago, Feb. 25--Elijah Muhammad, spiritual leader of the nation's Black Muslims, died here today of congestive heart failure.

The death of the 77-year-old "Messenger of Allah," as his followers called him, came as thousands of Muslims were gathering in Chicago for their biggest annual religious celebration, Saviors Day, scheduled for tomorrow.

Mr. Muhammad suffered from heart trouble, bronchitis, asthma and diabetes. He entered Mercy Hospital Jan. 30."

The following day after it was publically announced Elijah Muhammad died, the Nation of Islam held its annual Saviors Day

Convention is Chicago. All of the top labors spoke to pledge their support of his son, Wallace D. Muhammad, to lead.

When the National Representative of the Honorable Elijah Muhammad, Minister Louis Farrakhan, spoke, he offered these key points:

"He (Honorable Elijah Muhammad) taught us to submit to the will of All Mighty God Allah, and that is what makes us Muslim...His son is the will of God...Allah did not leave us comfortless, He gave us one from the Messengers family to comfort us...So we pray that All Mighty God Allah, in the name of the Messenger of Allah...that his son Wallace D. Muhammad will shoulder this mighty task, this mighty job, this mighty work of the resurrection of our people. And that we will offer all our resources....all our abilities to this son of the Messenger, in this divine work of the Messenger...

"And so I close,....we have learned the lesson of history that those who sit around waiting for fractions and split offs, waiting for those who would be hungry for leadership, hungry for power. I want you to know this afternoon that our father, Elijah Muhammad did not make that kind of people. The Honorable Elijah Muhammad lived for unity...And we today will keep that faith of Muhammad. And only in that faith will we find the unity and strength we need to help Minister Wallace D. Muhammad, the leader of the Nation of Islam carry on the noble work of his father....

"All of you that know the Messenger said one day his son would help him. That day has arrived and I like all the rest of Messenger Muhammad's followers submit and yield and give of myself all that I have within my power to see that the work for Messenger Muhammad is carried on to its completion behind the leadership of his son, the honorable Wallace D. Muhammad and the family of the Messenger....As Salaam Alaykum."[20]

These wise words, clearly indicate that the Honorable Elijah Muhammad's National Representative, Louis Farrakhan, pledged his support for Wallace D. Muhammad contingent upon him carrying out the mighty work of his father.

In 1975, Minister Farrakhan knew nothing about the FBI's 1969 file **Director, FBI (100-448006)** plan to destroy the Nation of Islam when it stated, *"In this connection Chicago should consider what counterintelligence action might be needed now or at the time of Elijah Muhammad's death to bring about such a change in NOI philosophy.*

---

[20] Youtube: 1975 Saviours Day – Imam W. Deen Mohammed 6

Important considerations should include the identity, strengths, and weaknesses, of any contenders for NOI leadership. <u>What are the positions of our [BUREAU DELETION] informants in regard to leadership? How could potential leaders be turned or neutralized?</u>"

Within one year after Saviour's Day, 1975 Wallace D. Muhammad removed Minister Louis Farrakhan as Minister over Harlem's Temple No. 7 and relocated him to a smaller Temple on the Westside of Chicago. And no, he was not ask to be a part of any advisory board to assist the new leadership. This was mainly due to the change in direction Wallace D. Muhammad was bringing about. Part of that change was none of the ministers were to teach Elijah Muhammad as the Messenger of Allah in which Minister Farrakhan resisted and ultimately rejected during the latter part of 1976. So he fell back, as the saying goes in the streets. In this manner, no public hostility or philosophical clashes occurred. Then again, they were related through marriage ties as some of his children were married some of Elijah Muhammad's sons and daughters. Therefore, in many respects, Minister Farrakhan was a spiritual son of the Honorable Elijah Muhammad while Wallace D. Muhammad was his physical son. Moreover, the Minister loved Wallace D. Muhammad as a son of his father, Elijah Muhammad like most of the members.

Nonetheless, at some point, instructions through Wallace D. Muhammad's leadership said for members of the Nation of Islam to throw away all books written by Elijah Muhammad. I reiterate, Minister Farrakhan did not know about the 1969 FBI file because it had not yet been released to the public via the freedom information act. However, the plan was being carried out like a script. This is not to say Wallace D. Muhammad was a government agent. No, the government agents were the men and women advising him as to how to transition away from his father's economic and spiritual policies, procedures and teachings.

"The alternative to changing the philosophy of the NOI is the destruction of the organization."[21]

Chapter 11

N.O.I. Destroyed Within 3 Years

Wallace D. Muhammad disbanded the original Nation of Islam (NOI) in 1976 and transformed it into an ostensibly orthodox mainstream Islamic movement, the Bilalians (1975), World Community of Al-Islam in the West (1976-77), the American Muslim Mission (1978-85,) which later became the American Society of Muslims.[22]

From a historical point of view, the day Wallace D. Muhammad planted the United States Flag of America inside the National Center of the Nation of Islam (Muhammad Temple No. 2), a great desecration repeated itself along the storyline of what the man **Antiochus IV Epiphanes** did in 167 BC. You ask, who is Antiochus

---

[21] Counterintelligence Program (FBI File Date: 01-07-1969)

[22] "The Emergence of Islam in the African-American Com)munity" Archived February 20, 2009, at the Wayback Machine

IV? Well let's begin with the meaning of his name i.e., God Manifest.

> There is an even more obscure answer. Antiochus IV (Epiphanes), the king of Syria, captured Jerusalem in 167 BC and desecrated the Temple by offering the sacrifice of a pig on an altar to Zeus (the Abomination of Desolation). In seeking to prohibit Judaism and Hellenize the Jews, Antiochus forbade their religious practices and commanded that copies of the Law be burned, all of which is related by Josephus in the *Antiquities of the Jews* (XII.5.4).
>
>> "...he [Antiochus] got possession of the city by treachery; at which time he spared not so much as those that admitted him into it, on account of the riches that lay in the temple; but, led by his covetous inclination, (for he saw there was in it a great deal of gold, and many ornaments that had been dedicated to it of very great value,) and in order to plunder its wealth, he ventured to break the league he had made. So he left the temple bare, and took away the golden candlesticks, and the golden altar, and table, and the altar; and did not abstain from even the veils, which were made of fine linen and scarlet. He also emptied it of its secret treasures, and left nothing at all remaining; and by this means cast the Jews into great lamentation, for he forbade them to offer those daily sacrifices which they used to offer to God, according to the law.

None the wiser, history has a way of repeating itself. In the case of the Nation of Islam, it had entered into a fulfilment of time just like all Black people whose forbearers endured 400 years of slavery throughout the western hemisphere thereby fulfilling role as the children of Israel.

By 1980, Wallace D. Muhammad, now known as Imam W. Deen Mohammed released a book entitled *"As The Light Shineth From The East."* A part of his objective was to explain to the former members of the Nation of Islam how his father was not really teaching true Islam and that the person, Master Fard Muhammad, who original founded the Nation of Islam in 1930 and taught his father Elijah Muhammad was a witch doctor of sorts. (See Appendix i, Master Fard Muhammad)

By now, of course, Minister Louis Farrakhan had long taken himself away from under the leadership of Imam W. Deen Mohammed. His work was no longer carrying out the work of Elijah Muhammad. The great opposition against the teachings of the Honorable Elijah Muhammad and everything he stood for had reached the Rubicon. So one might say Minister Farrakhan remained true to his wise choice of words spoken Saviour's Day 1975.

"So we pray that All Mighty God Allah, in the name of the Messenger of Allah...that his son Wallace D. Muhammad will shoulder this mighty task, this mighty job, this mighty work of the resurrection of our people. And that we will offer all

our resources....all our abilities to this son of the Messenger, in this divine work of the Messenger..."[23]

The issues "Wallace D. Muhammad had against his father were both personal and scriptural (or philosophical). The issues Minister Louis Farrakhan had with Imam W. Deen Mohammed were scriptural (or philosophical), not personal. In 1976, early 1977, an idea began to rise in his heart to lift the name of Elijah Muhammad and to rebuild his work.[24] However, he did not carry this idea out. At that time, it was merely a great desire.

Chapter 12

Farrakhan Rebuild Nation of Islam 1977

When Minister Louis Farrakhan took himself from beneath the leadership of Imam W. Deen Mohammed, the Headquarters of the Nation of Islam was deposed by a brand new structure called, "World Community of Al-Islam in the West". Therefore, in 1976 or 1977, rebuilding the Nation of Islam was not initially on the forefront of his mind, yet it sparkled in his heart's desire. Since he could not teach anymore, going back into show business was the foremost practical way to take care of his family, thought the Minister.

---

[23] Saviour's Day February 1975
[24] Final Call April 24, 2014: Allah, His precise time, purpose and glory by Jabril Muhammad

"He wanted to decide what he should do. He contacted football legend and actor, Jim Brown, in Los Angeles, and stayed there." [25]

At some point, while in Los Angeles, he contacted a certain brother whom he had known in Temple No. 11, Boston. The brother was an entertainment promoter.

"During this time he was still considering entertainment and began to meet individually with entertainers to gauge their thoughts on the matter...He met with actors, Brock Peters, Bernie Casey, Jayne Kennedy, singer Smokey Robinson and writers Maya Angelou and James Balwin".

After several meetings, rather than going back to singing, as his friends thought entertainment would be beneath him, he came up with the idea writing and starring a movie about Malcolm X since he personally knew him.

Considering this historical background, the Minister did not set out to make a split off group in 1977. There was nothing to split off from. The foundation of the original Nation of Islam had been destroyed. He did not come to realize he would rebuild the work of the Honorable Elijah Muhammad until September 1977 after his encounter with Barnard Cushmeer, the brother whom was born in the same hospital as he was born and also a former drummer. A drummer out of Bronx, New York. As all good

---

[25] Final Call Newspaper, October 2003 A True Pioneer Pt. 2

drummers know, there role is to keep time. All drummers must have a sensitive ear, a good sense of timing and memory of the song.

Recall earlier in this book, it was said Brother Cushmeer, for several years during the 1960's, resided with Elijah Muhammad. He was being specially trained, scripturally, to one day function as Elijah Muhammad's envoy for a future event or meeting. Unbeknownst to himself, in 1965, that event or meeting was to come to pass September 1977 in Los Angeles, California.

Historically speaking, Barnard Cushmeer had last spoke with Minister Farrakhan in December 1974, but was prevented speaking about what was on his mind.

"I wanted to talk to him, but I could not, like I wanted to. For one reason, others were always present. My time was limited" [26]

Then in February 1975 he spoke again, but could not say anything about what had occurred on February 25th.

"That was a closer call, but such a meeting was yet to come."

For three years, Cushmeer had no idea of the Ministers whereabouts. One day, while seeking to find his brother, Cushmeer was made aware that Minister Farrakhan was in the

---

[26] Final Call April 24, 2014: Allah, His precise time, purpose and glory by Jabril Muhammad

City of Angels (Los Angeles). So he headed out West. His intention was to meet and to give him some reading material that dealt with a letter Elijah Muhammad sent to him in 1966 among other scriptural realities.

The brother who witnessed this encounter between CUSHMEER and FARRAKHAN is now named Abdul Wahid Muhammad pictured to the right. Brother Wahid was the one helping Minister Farrakhan, in Los Angeles, setting up interviews preparing for the Malcolm X movie. Brother Wahid

Abdul Wahid Muhammad

would schedule appointments and bring various actors to the Ministers makeshift office at the Hyatt Hotel located on Sunset Blvd.

"We set up our office in the restaurant of the Hyatt Hotel…I acted as the receptionist and went to greet people as they entered the restaurant. I guided them back our office booth."
27

One day, on a Friday, Brother Cushmeer arrived at the hotel. He was carrying two brown paper bags that he wanted to give to the Minister. So Brother Wahid informed Minister Farrakhan about Brother Cushmeer's arrival. They both went into a restaurant to eat and talk in private. The main mission of

---

27 **Final Call Newspaper, October 2003 A True Pioneer Pt. 2**

Barnard Cushmeer's purpose was to get the Minister to read the material he had brought with him. For all intents and purposes, the material given to Minister Farrakhan by Brother Cushmeer clarified some divine Biblical and Quranic scriptures dealing with Jesus escaping a death plot and how it all related to the life and times of the Honorable Elijah Muhammad. Or as Minister Farrakhan said:

"[It] chronicles the life of Jesus and compares it to the life of the Honorable Elijah Muhammad, and the rise and fall of the Nation to the rise and fall of the early church when Jesus went to the cross" [28]

It took Minister Farrakhan three days to read the material. On the third day, Sunday, Cushmeer came back to see the Minister. Brother Wahid was also present. He looked at the Minister and said:

"...whatever he was planning on doing that I wanted to be a part of it. The said that he was going to rebuild the Teachings of the Honorable Elijah Muhammad." [29]

---

[28] Ibid A True Pioneer Pt. 2

[29] Ibid A True Pioneer Pt. 2

Farrakhan Muhammad soon ask Brother Wahid to move to Chicago. Once in Chicago, it was there in the home of the Farrakhan family where the rebuilding work proceeded 24/7. So in many respects, Abdul Wahid Muhammad was Minister Farrakhan's first follower in 1977. As well, Barnard Cushmeer was like and angel merely delivering a message. The timing could not

(l front) Barnard Cushmeer)   *(r front) Hon. Minister Louis Farrakhan*

have been better. That is to say, FARRAKHAN had been denied from doing the work of the Honorable Elijah Muhammad in just under three years from 1975 to 1977. When Cushmeer reached Farrakhan with the material he learned from the Honorable Elijah Muhammad during the 1960's, the Directors, FBI (100-448006) plan was foiled. Allah's plan was the best plan! HAsatan could not have FARRAKHAN!

Chapter 13
Farrakhan's Great Announcement

It took Minister Farrakhan six years (1975 – 1981) to bring back the Nation of Islam's Saviour's Day Conventions from the year it was announced the Honorable Elijah Muhammad died. Saviour's Day 1981 was the year of Jubilee once Minister Farrakhan announced the Honorable Elijah Muhammad was in fact alive and had escaped a death plot on February 25, 1975. The context and content of the material Cushmeer gave him in 1977 which triggered him to make such an announcement is now in book form entitled *"Is It Possible That The Honorable Elijah Muhammad is Physically Alive"*. What you can read in this book is the material Brother Barnard Cushmeer gave to Minister Louis Farrakhan September 1977. The book is a way to understand what has been hidden heretofore by Rome to keep Black people from taking their rightful place on earth. It makes clear to those who may be none the wiser, along with other detailed exegesis, who is who and what is what. You'll also read the letter Elijah Muhammad gave to Cushmeer in 1966 that says in part:

"if Allah had not shown me how I was going to escape, I would have no hope."

What the general public did not understand nor discern is that Elijah Muhammad engineered the fall and rise of the Nation of Islam according to how his Teacher, Master Fard Muhammad, revealed it to him beginning in 1931. He revealed a divine plan to assure the Nation of Islam would be released from captivity by its enemies plan. By means of the positioning of certain people, family members (including his son), and ministers to fulfill a variety of roles, the Nation would rise from its ashes.

Fact is, Master Fard Muhammad taught Elijah Muhammad how to decode and apply the entire volume of scripture (Bible and Quran). Can it be proven? Yes! The meeting between Cushmeer and Farrakhan—the High Priest, was planned and executed; biblically! Overcoming the FBI and other counterintelligence programs to prevent the rise of Elijah Muhammad's "philosophy" is of Biblical proportions.

Take for instance the history of Joshua, the High Priest of Moses. Theologically speaking, Joshua (Hebrew *Yəhōšuaʿ*) the High Priest was, according to the Bible, the first person chosen to be the High Priest for the reconstruction of the Jewish Temple, after the return of the Jews from the Babylonian Captivity. In fulfillment of Joshua's foreshadowed history, *illustration i* is the second version Temple No. 2 recaptured, in 1988, by the Honorable Minister Louis Farrakhan, and members of the Nation of Islam. It was reconstructed and renamed Mosque Maryam in 1989 to demonstrate to Allah's enemies that He is the best of planners; Sovereign Owner of Everything.

Talmudic Jews Vs Farrakhan 1984

In 1984 Reverend Jesse Jackson had become a viable candidate for office of Presidency of the United States and therefore began receiving multiple death threats; namely, from certain members of the Jewish sector. There main gripe against him was due to his fair and balanced political position with respect to the Palestinians and Israelis land disputes.

As part of his position stated:

"In the Middle East, Israeli security/Palestinian self-determination are two sides of the same coin. We must do for them what they cannot do for each other: break the cycle of violence, provide guarantees for mutual security in exchange for mutual recognition, land in exchange for peace."[30]

Saviour's Day 1981 + 7 years = 1988, the year Minister Farrakhan recaptured Muhammad's Temple #2. The following year, 1989, he cleansed it, so to speak and renamed it Mosque Maryam, the 2nd version. Thus fulfilling the recurrence of the ancient Maccabean Revolt of 176 BC to 160 BC as told and prophesied by our ancient Christian Ethiopic brothers and sisters. (See Appendix i, Ethiopian Bible)

To people of good will, Mr. Jackson's position was humane. But to some Jews, this was meddling into their affairs. Therefore, an anti-Jesse Jackson campaign was initiated.

---

[30] By **Demetric Muhammad, Guest Columnist** August 11, 2020 Final Call Newspaper

"A group called Jews Against Jackson, an offshoot of the radical Jewish Defense League that has been disavowed by leaders of most Jewish organizations, pledged publicly to disrupt his candidacy. Two of its members were arrested for interrupting his announcement speech on Nov. 3 in Washington, D.C. A window in Jackson's New Hampshire campaign headquarters in Manchester was smashed, and his campaign offices in Garden Grove, Calif., were firebombed. Jackson's life has been threatened."[31]

These events compelled the Honorable Minister Louis Farrakhan to place the F.O.I. as security around Jesse Jackson, his family and campaign offices throughout the country. Then on February 25, 1984 the Minister delivered the following words to the public:

"I say to you as intelligent people, sit down and talk with Rev. Jackson. Sit down Jewish leaders and talk with us. We are ready to talk with you. Sit down and talk like intelligent people who have a future at stake. But if you harm this brother, I warn you in the name of Allah, this will be the last one you harm. We are not making any idle threats, we have no weapons, we [don't] carry so much as a pen knife. But I do tell the world that Almighty God Allah is backing us up in what we say and what we do, and we warn you in His name—leave this servant of Almighty God alone. Leave him alone. If you want to defeat him, defeat him at the polls. We can stand to lose an election, but we cannot stand to lose our brother. ..."

---

[31] March 12, 1984 Time Magazine

From that day, February 25, 1984 forward, a party of powerful Jews working the **methodeía**[32] of Satan have set out to destroy the Honorable Minister Louis Farrakhan's repetition and even take his life. Why? Because he has not and will bend his will to their will (way of thinking).

To show their hand, on February 27, 1984, Nathan Pearlmutter of the Anti-Defamation League of B'nai B'rith (ADL) referred to Minister Farrakhan as a new *"Black Hitler."* Next, Nat Hentoff, a Jewish leader and columnist for the tabloid Village

---

[32] method used in organized evil-doing (well-crafted trickery)

Voice participated in a New York radio call-in show and also characterized the Muslim leader as a *"Black Hitler."*

The worst insult made by modern day Jewish scribes is what the Jewish Bulletin printed. (See Hitler sitting up top Minster Farrakhan's shoulders). Such rotten tactics only demonstrated a continuum of divine history unfolding again. That is: The controversy between Jesus and the ruling and/or influential Jews 2000 years ago being played out in North America. It's obvious, the picture was designed to ruin Minister Farrakhan's

repetition and character. However, it did not work. The he went on to speak to multitudes, hundreds and thousands of Black men, women and children across America. In 1985 he addressed 35,000 at New York's Madison Square Garden.

Before arriving to his New York event, he had attracted large audiences in Los Angeles, Washington, Baltimore and other cities by the thousands. And at every step along the way, the Jewish press attacked his character attempting to keep people away. For example, before the Minister arrived in New York, the New York Times printed the following article:

FARRAKHAN PLANS RALLY AT GARDEN; KOCH ASSAILS HIM AS ANTI-SEMITE

By Robert D. McFadden
Sept. 23, 1985

"The Rev. Louis Farrakhan, the Black Muslim whose attacks on Judaism have been rebuked by Jewish leaders and others, plans to discuss black economic and political power at a rally at Madison Square Garden on Oct. 7, a spokesman said yesterday.

Mayor Koch, accusing Mr. Farrakhan of engaging in "the vilest of anti-Semitism" at similar rallies in Washington and Los Angeles recently, called on leaders of all religious and ethnic groups to "denounce" Mr. Farrakhan, "his racism and his religious bigotry."

Before New York, though, he spoke in Los Angeles, California to a crowd of 20,000 people. Afterwards, the Los Angeles Times printed the following article:

Farrakhan Case--Will Jewish Voters Abandon Bradley in '86?

By KEITH LOVE
OCT. 13, 1985 12 AM PT
TIMES POLITICAL WRITER

Mayor Tom Bradley's handling last month of an appearance by black Muslim Louis Farrakhan probably set back Bradley's effort to recast his image as he prepares to run for governor in 1986, according to some Democratic strategists.

It remains to be seen, however, how badly Bradley hurt himself with Jews, a group that has always been crucial to his political success.

Before the incident over Farrakhan's Sept. 14 speech in Inglewood, the usually low-key Bradley had begun to present a more active and decisive image as he moved toward a rematch with Republican Gov. George Deukmejian next year. Bradley's actions ranged from rafting down the Kern River to telling city pension fund officers to begin divestiture from South Africa or risk dismissal.

California Democratic activists and Jewish leaders interviewed recently agreed, however, that Bradley's image-remaking probably suffered during the Farrakhan incident."

Louis Farrakhan Theology of Music 1993

In 1993, the Honorable Minister Louis Farrakhan celebrated his 60th birthday by performing a Violin Mendelssohn

Concerto conducted by Michael Morgan, assistant conductor of the Chicago Symphony Orchestra. The concert was held in Winston Salem N.C. April 18. It was, in the highest spiritual sense, a form of worship to bring about healing to human beings.

The humanity of the Ministers intentions eased many Black people of high rank in American professional, clergy, political and business folks, including members of the entertainment society. Conversely, Abraham Foxman, national director of the Anti-Defamation League of B'nai B'rith had this to say:

"Playing the music of dead Jews will not repair the depth of hurt, insult and damage that the Rev. Louis Farrakhan's mouth has spewed forth," he said, regarding Farrakhan's musical outreach.

"I wouldn't dignify his gimmick by calling it outreach. This man has said vile things, not to one person but on platforms, and every time he is challenged, he uses the shabbiest verbal acrobatics to try to explain it away.

"It's hard to say what one has to do after all that to make amends, but I think he can begin with an apology."[33]

---

[33] Chicago Tribune By Clarence Page April 28, 1993   Washington

After performing in Winston, Salem his next violin concert was held in Chicago, Illinois Christ Universal Temple as a fund raiser for the Nation of Islam scholarship fund. Inside the Christ Universal Temple, members of the church community and Nation of Islam were celebrating listening to castanets, harps, lyres, tumbrels, sistrums and cymbals under the command Minister Farrakhan's stringed instrument—his violin.

What did the managing editor for Making Music Magazine, Jason say about Minister Farrakhan's violin abilities?

"The long-time leader of the Nation of Islam may not be the first famous person who comes to mind when you think of non-professional violin players, but Louis Farrakhan is a skilled violinist."

In 2016, Minster Farrakhan released his long awaited album, "Lets Change The World". This was a 14-year project, recorded in 16 studios across the country including Mosque Maryam in Chicago. ***"It's 45 songs in every genre you can imagine,"*** said Min. Farrakhan. The project includes classical, gospel and jazz, folk, opera,

rap, reggae and calypso. *"So, it was my life's journey in music,"* said Min. Farrakhan...[34]

[34] www.noi.org/farrakhan-music/

Bay State Banner magazine gave the album nothing but praise for the performance and performers on the Ministers album.

Farrakhan's masterful album set to change the world

Melvin B. Miller

Farrakhan's "Let's Save the World" album contains a number of recordings that he has produced and have now been compiled as a gift of love to all humanity. His understanding of the power of music is that "the science of music ... is at the root of the true religion of God." So now, after his 60-year mission to resurrect the black man and woman from their long travails in America, Farrakhan has presented a seven-disc collection of music to help lift all human beings to a higher spiritual level.

The first piece, "Salut d'Amour" (Greetings of Love) by Edward Elgar, recorded in 2013, establishes his musical intention. Then his performance of J.S. Bach's "Double Violin Concerto" with Ayke Agos clearly assures the listener of his competence to perform technically at the highest level. His production of the Londonderry Air, an Irish folk song, then establishes the universality of Farrakhan's call to save the world.

The variety of artist appearing on the Album speaks volumes. Minister Farrakhan's role in divine history as the fulfiller of the Lords musician commanding thousands of instruments is evident. Just to name a few, the list of artist reads:

- Snoop Dogg
- Chaka Khan
- Rapper, Rick Ross
- Damian Marley (Bob Marley's son)
- Stephanie Mills,
- Common, Chaka Khan,
- Tina Maria
- Steve Wonder
- Charles Veal
- Sylvia Olden Lee
- Karen Briggs and dozens other great musical legends were on his album

His admiration among the entertainers, brothers and sisters in the streets and professionals is one the world's best kept secrets. While the haters, jealous minded and religious hypocrites promote lies, by the look of these photos, the question is: Who is the Honorable Minister Louis Farrakhan through the lens of righteous heart people?

Million Man March 1995

1995 served noticed to all enemies of the Honorable Minister Louis Farrakhan and the God he serves that greater is he in him than in the world of white Authority and/or methodia of Satan to stop him. His scheduling across the country had set the stage for the biggest gathering ever, in Washington D.C. The overwhelming event was termed the Million Man March (MMM)

This march did not merely happen. Minister Farrakhan traveled hundreds and thousands of miles across America speaking with his people in churches, stadiums, college campuses and what not. He laid a foundation, made the call; and, nearly 2 million Black men descended upon Washington, D.C., on October 16, 1995. It was a Day of Atonement, reconciliation and responsibility. Numerous notable speakers represented their "tribes". All 12 tribes of Israel!

See List of Notable speakers, organizers and elders

- Marion Barry, Mayor of Washington, D.C. – "Mayor's Welcome and Official Statement"
- Cora Masters Barry, First Lady, District of Columbia – Mistress of Ceremonies
- Dr. Betty Shabazz – remarks
- Minister Rasul Muhammad and Minister Ishmael Muhammad – Master of Ceremonies
- Reverend Benjamin Chavis – National Director of Million Man March – Call to Purpose
- Martin Luther King III – Affirmation of our Brothers
- Rosa Parks – Mothers of the Struggle Behold Thy Sons
- Maya Angelou – Appeal to Our Brothers
- Reverend Jeremiah Wright – Prayer for Hope
- Dr. Maulana Karenga – Mission statement for the Million Man March/National Day of Absence
- Senator Adelbert Bryan – Senator, Virgin Islands
- Rev. James Bevel – The Theological Foundation for Atonement
- Reverend Jesse L. Jackson Sr. – Rainbow/PUSH Coalition
- Reverend Addis Daniel – The Light
- Rev. H. Beecher Hicks of Washington

- Sheik Ahmed Tijani Ben-Omar of Accra, Ghana
- Rev. Frederick Haynes, III from the Friendship West Baptist Church, Dallas, Texas –
- Rev. Wayne Gadie of the Emanuel Baptist Church, Malden, Massachusetts –
- Opening prayer Dancers and drummers from the village of Kankoura, Burkina Faso
- Greetings from the African Diaspora from the continent of Africa and the Caribbean
- Greetings from Black American leaders such as George Augustus Stallings, Oscar Easton (Blacks in Government)
- Henry Nichols (Hospital Workers Union),
- Dr. Niam Akbar (Florida State University)
- Zachery McDaniels (National African American Leadership Summit)
- Rev. Willie F. Wilson of Union Temple Baptist Church, Washington, D.C.,
- Rev. Al Sampson, Fernwood United Methodist Church (Chicago) – "A Declaration of Purpose"
- Boubacar Joseph Ndiaye, Chief Curator Goree Island (Senegal) – "The African Diaspora"
- Congressman Donald M. Payne, Chair, Congressional Black Caucus – "The Congress"
- Former Congressman Gus Savage – "The Statesman"
- Kurt Schmoke, Mayor of Baltimore, Maryland – "The Cities"
- Martin Luther King III – remarks
- Tynnetta Muhammad – remarks
- Faye Williams, attorney – Washington, D.C. coordinator Million Man March
- Dorothy I. Height
- Bishop H. H. Brookins of the 5th Episcopal District, AME in Los Angeles, California – the prayer for atonement

- Rev. James Bevel – the Theological Foundation for Atonement
- Dr. Cornel West – Statement of Atonement
- Rev. Joseph Lowery – Statement of Atonement[35]

The Honorable Minister Louis Farrakhan spoke last but not least. His demonstration of the journey leading up to the Million Man March was the greatest example of Black Power sense Mansa Musa made his journey across the Sahara Desert into Egypt, 1334 AD, and then on into Mecca, Arabia.

How did the Jewish press see the Million Man March?

Jewish Press Respond to Million Man March

October 15, 1995 what how did the Jewish press respond to the Million Man March?

News Analysis: Million Man March Poses Dilemma for Future Black-jewish Relations

OCTOBER 15, 1995 4:00 AM

This week's Million Man March has catapulted Farrakhan to the forefront of the African American community and has secured him the seat he long has coveted at the table of black leadership. "Louis Farrakhan has gained legitimacy and captured the limelight," said Abraham Foxman, national director of the Anti- Defamation League, who in the weeks preceding the march was the Jewish community's most vocal critic of its leadership.

---

[35] Million Man March - Wikipedia

Murray Friedman, author of a book on black-Jewish relations and a former vice chairman of the U.S. Civil Rights Commission, agreed. "Farrakhan has now found a way of koshering himself with the black community," Friedman said. Farrakhan's rehabilitation has thrown new doubts on the future of already strained black-Jewish relations.

"Should Louis Farrakhan emerge as a leader of the black community, that would be a problem that cannot be understated," said Lawrence Rubin, executive vice chairman of the National Jewish Community Relations Advisory Council.
"It would be impossible for members of the Jewish community to sit down with members of the black community if Farrakhan were included," Rubin said.

In fact, that very scenario has already occurred in Washington. A member of the local American Jewish Committee and a local rabbi publicly and loudly resigned from Mayor Marion Barry's religious advisory committee when officials invited Nation of Islam representatives to participate....

Friedman said, referring to the most difficult economic and social issues facing African Americans. "It may very well be that blacks and Jews need a pause from each other," he said.
But there is a line which Foxman strongly urged the black community not to cross. "If Farrakhan becomes part of the package I will not sit at the table," he said. "We will not sit with a bigot to fight bigotry. We will not sit with a racist to fight racism.

I don't know about you, but the undertone and overtone of Jewish leadership sounds as if they own Black Americas decision-making-process when it comes to receiving Minister Louis Farrakhan in their presence. Nevertheless, no matter what they accused FARRAKHAN of being, in 1995 he showed their weakness. And that is the old political Jewish guard did not want to lose total influence over the old Black leaderships total mind.

Chapter 14

Farrakhan's 3 World Tours

The Honorable Minister Louis Farrakhan has taken the message and teachings of the Most Honorable Elijah Muhammad around the world. He has helped his brother and friend, just as Elijah asked Allah for a helper during Saviour's Day 1954.

Not only did Elijah's Minister travel throughout North America delivering the message of salvation and restoration to awaken Black America—the real Children of Israel and/or Islam, he also took 3 world tours of duty to demonstrate the power of the message of the Honorable Elijah Muhammad and the True and Living God. Who else protected FARRAHAN during his travels, for no ordinary man could have carried out the mission accomplished as did Elijah's Minister without Divine Protection from a Divine Supreme Being.

. The success of the Million Man March (MMM) set the stage for Minister Louis Farrakhan's world tours. African and Muslims nations wanted to see and hear directly from the man who united every Black organization to participate at the historical event in Washington D.C. So a few months after the MMM, he set out on a World Friendship Tour. Among the first countries visited were:

- South Africa
- Libya
- Sudan
- Nigeria
- Syria.

In all, he and his delegation of brothers and sisters attended 3 World Tours after the Million Man March which further included tour stops in:

- Iran (for an Islamic Conference)
- Iraq
- Kuwait
- The United Arab Emirates
- Saudi Arabia
- Israel
- Palestine
- China
- Malaysia
- Singapore
- 20 countries in Africa
- Libya,
- North Korea
- South Korea
- The former Soviet Union
- Siberia
- Daghestan in the Caucasus Mountains.
- Nations in the South Pacific, the Caribbean and South America

The photos you are about to view is proof positive that governmental officials of other nations recognized the Honorable Minister Louis Farrakhan as a divine servant of God and some saw him as Allah's servant in their mist. Many of those world leaders understood that if Allah's Divine Power was not backing FARRAKHAN, he could not have entered into their countries and exited safe and sound. For the hidden political powers that impede even their own governmental progress surely desired to kill him for telling the gospel TRUTH.

Al-Azhar University
Cairo, Egypt December 1997
Bamako, Mali December 1997
Independence Stadium
Banjul, The Gambia December 1997

Azadi Square
Tehran, Iran February 1996
(to a crowd of 6 to 7 million)
Sudan University
Khartoum, Sudan January 1998
Palace of the Oba (King) of Benin
Benin City, Nigeria February 1996

Central Mosque of Moscow
Moscow, Russia *January 1998*

Mosque Al Nur
Damascus, Syria *July 2002*

Reception in Seoul, Korea February 1998
Hosted by Rev. Sun Myung Moon

Mosque Amir El Mouminine
Sydney, Australia February 1998

Libya Offers 1 Billion Dollars To N.O.I.

Nineteen years from the time the Honorable Minister Louis Farrakhan stood up to rebuild the work of the Honorable Elijah Muhammad, the Islamic government of Libya, in 1996, offered to him and the Nation of Islam $1 Billion dollars. The cost to mobilize the oppressed people of America is far above that amount. But such an offer demonstrated the Ministers global impact and value.

But, on August 27, 1996 News Nation/World reported concerning the matter of Minister Farrakhan and $1 billion dollars from Libya.

"The Nation of Islam is seeking official permission to collect the $1 billion, which would require a waiver of strict U.S. sanctions against transactions with Libya. Lawyers also are seeking permission for Farrakhan to travel soon to Tripoli, the capital, to accept a $250,000 humanitarian award from Gadhafi.

"Farrakhan's requests create an election-year quandary for the White House, which is anxious not to alienate African-American voters but remains wary of frequent Republican criticism that President Clinton lacks foreign policy backbone.

"We don't think much of Libya, and there are things about the Reverend Farrakhan's travels that we don't think much of, as well," said White House spokesman Mike McCurry as the presidential campaign train made a stop in Arlington, Ohio. "And obviously we expect U.S. citizens to obey the law." In Washington, a State

Department official reminded reporters of the administration's strong criticism of Farrakhan in January, when he visited Libya, Iraq, Iran, Nigeria and other pariah states. Spokesman Nicholas Burns said at the time that Farrakhan was "cavorting with dictators....

"Farrakhan has made clear that he will fight to accept Libya's money. Amid the firestorm earlier this year, he dared the U.S. government to prevent him from receiving Libyan money. He said he was ready for a "showdown."

"Farrakhan said he would not be a Libyan agent: "I am an agent of God, and if the government requests that I should register as an agent of God, I will be happy to do so."

According to the Wall Street Journal, who also chimed in on the $1 billion dollar donation, Dorothy J. GaiterStaff Reporter of The Wall Street Journal on Aug. 26, 1996, wrote:

"People close to the planning expect that if the $1 billion is actually received, about $400 million of it would be invested in black-, Hispanic- and Arab-owned banks so they can make more loans in their communities. A little more than that $400 million would be put under management of one Hispanic-owned and five black-owned investment firms to encourage corporate executives to adhere to social and economic policies that are helpful to minorities, an insider says. The remainder would support the Nation of Islam's operations, underwrite a foundation, fund voter-registration efforts and pay Mr. Harris's fees, the insider says."

In the final close, the United States Governmental officials, by legal fiction, prevented the $1 billion dollar donation to the Nation of Islam under Minister Farrakhan's leadership.

(Left) President Rawlings of Ghana, (Middle) Minister Louis Farrakhan, (Far right Col. Muammar Gaddafi)

Farrakhan Battles For His Health 1999

In 1999, Minister Farrakhan had entered into Howard University Hospital for surgery to treat what had been on going health issue since 1991.Rumors were swirling, *'who is going to take over to replace Farrakhan.'*

The New York Post released the following news flash.

NEWS

NATION OF ISLAM SAYS FARRAKHAN IS CLOSE TO DEATH

By Gersh Kuntzman

March 18, 1999 | 5:00am

Minister Louis Farrakhan — firebrand leader of the Nation of Islam — is near death with a mysterious illness, his group's official newspaper says.

...Nation officials in Chicago and New York did not return calls yesterday.

This week's Village Voice, quoting an unnamed Nation of Islam source, reports that Farrakhan believes he was poisoned — possibly by government agents.

"The Minister says he knows who [poisoned him], he knows where, and he knows why," the Voice source said. "He just doesn't know what [was used to] poison him."

The sensationalism behind Minister Farrakhan entering into the hospital made many of his detractors happy with glee. The worst form of such glee was illustrated in the cartoon image below. His nemeses never expected him to come out alive. But he came out alive.

DOCTORS DESPERATELY TRY TO REMOVE THE CANCEROUS TUMOR FROM FARRAKHAN'S BODY

Many people do not know, the physical pain he has endured in the continuum of the work of the Most Honorable Elijah Muhammad's to restore those who will to be restored and comprehend the gospel truth. In spite of his operations and internal scares it caused to his body, his beautiful spirit continued to radiate joy.

Farrakhan Performs Violin Concerto 2002

To the surprise of so many people, Minister Farrakhan was holding the Nation of Islam's annual Saviours' Day Convention in Los Angeles, California. Before the main event, he performed a musical benefit to raise funds for Muhammad's University of Islam. The concert was held in Cerritos, California Center for the Performing Arts to a crowd of nearly 1,700 people. His performance *"The Beethoven Violin Concerto"* was spell bounding. Who was is the audience?

"Dignitaries in the audience included Imam Warith Deen Mohammed, leader of the Muslim American Society, singer Jermaine Jackson, entrepreneur Karl Kani, actor Michael Colyer, Martin Luther King III, L.A. Police Chief Bernard Parks and former D.C. Mayor Marion Barry and wife Cora.

"In an interview with The Final Call, Imam Mohammed said, "This is heavenly right here. I am really proud to be a friend and a brother of Minister Farrakhan. I'm not one to judge when it comes to the

classics, but what came across to my ears tonight sounded beautiful."[36]

As you may realize, Imam W. Deen Mohammed and Minister Louis Farrakhan had reconciled many differences since the year 1975. After all, they were related through marriage ties. So once again, Black history was made to overcome the old past histories, in particularly, between the Muslims of the Middle East

Imam W. Deen Mohammed and Minister Farrakhan Saviours' Day 2000

who have been at war with one another from the time of the Arabia prophet, Muhammad Ibn Abdullah's passing, Peace Be Upon Him. But, with respect to Minister Farrakhan and Imam W. Deen Mohammed, no bloodshed has been spilled between their

---

[36] Final Call Newspaper WEB POSTED 02-25-2002

adherents going back to Saviour's Day 1975. Henceforward, prophecy was fulfilled in the fullness of our time.

Anti-Farrakhan Machine Failed 2020

In spite of all the love Minister Louis Farrakhan has received and spread too many nations across the planet, his number one nemesis continue to twist his message of restoration. Their limited brains does not comprehend that Black people carry the original Semitic DNA down into their bone morrow. Alright now! Smile.

After reading the HEADLINES NEWS article released on July 15, 2020 by the *Anti-Defamation League (ADL),* formerly known as the Anti-Defamation League of B'nai B'rith, which is an international Jewish non-governmental organization based in the United States, ask two questions to yourself: (a) what is their intention? (b) Who is the Honorable Minister Louis Farrakhan?

ANTISEMITISM IN THE US

EXTREMISM, TERRORISM & BIGOTRY
Farrakhan Remains Most Popular Antisemite in America
July 15, 2020

Nation of Islam Never Fall Again 2021

What the reader must come to comprehend is that Master Fard Muhammad revealed to Elijah Muhammad how to understand how both scripts (Bible and Quran). Each contain Black America's divine history as well. Not only Jewish and Arab history can be read in scriptures. Remember that!

Earlier in this book, it was stated that the Honorable Elijah Muhammad engineered the fall and rise of the Nation of Islam. He did so by setting the stage for his son, Wallace D. Muhammad, to do God's Manifest i.e., take control over the N.O.I. and destroy the Temple structure. Afterward, it would be rebuilt. Then we wrote, while at the same time, as early as 1965, he was preparing Barnard Cushmeer (now known as Jabril Muhammad) to retrieve Minister Louis Farrakhan after his falling away due to what had occurred on February 25, 1975. And what had occurred? Farrakhan believed the Honorable Elijah Muhammad passed away. So principally, what Jabril Muhammad carried out was what was written by Luke of the Bible, Luke 22:32: *"But I have made prayer for you that your faith may not give out; and you, once you have returned, strengthen your brothers."*

Ever since the year 1977, Louis Gene Walcott (Minister Louis Farrakhan) born through Sister Sarah Mae (**Princess Mary**), has been fulfilling his portion of divine scripture.

Why has the Honorable Minister Louis Farrakhan soared like a bird above and beyond all of his enemies? Why is he loved by millions across the planet earth? What manner of man is he that does not have one petty jealous bone in his body? It is due to his access to a fountain of knowledge? Thankfully, now that he has been strengthening his brethren going on 44 years (1977 + 44 years = 2021), he has been engineering the Nation of Islam to never fall again.

I reiterate, he has and is engineering the Nation's structural integrity to never fall, collapse or be not overthrown. Individuals may come and go, but the staff of Farrakhan is likened to the staff of Aaron. Why, because in the hearts of his staff is inscribed the name **FARRAKHAN**!

The production of time belonging to him, we can say goes back 66 years from today. (1955 + 66 years = 2021) The lessons he had learned from his early days in Boston as a captain and minister were vitally necessary. Consequently, he was able to deal with Harlem, New York's rebuilding efforts, as the National Representative of the Honorable Elijah Muhammad, after Malcolm X. Such production of time in shaping **FARRAKAHN** is why he was the man capable and skilled enough to rebuild the Nation of Islam beginning from nothing. And he did it with joy and pain.

In summary, it is easy to tell, Minister Farrakhan was produced from the mind of the Black nation and now he has meticulously schooled his staff, laborers and adherents not to fall for any of HAsatan's tricks upon his taking-leave.

And 'on Judgment Day' Allah will say, "O Jesus, son of Mary! Remember My favour upon you and your mother: how I supported you with the holy spirit[1] so you spoke to people in 'your' infancy and adulthood. How I taught you writing, wisdom, the Torah, and the Gospel. How you moulded a bird from clay—by My Will—and breathed into it and it became a 'real' bird—by My Will. How you healed the blind and the lepers—by My Will. How you brought the dead to life—by My Will. How I prevented the Children of Israel from harming you when you came to them with clear proofs and the disbelievers among them said, "This is nothing but pure magic."

Holy Quran 5:110

He is blessed to have spoken to the people from his youth to his old age. For what it's all worth, The Honorable Minister Louis Farrakhan has proven for this generation that the mystery of God is finished!

Quran and Return Of Jesus

Of all the divine servants of Allah, why did Prophet Muhammad of Arabia, born 570 years after Jesus tell the Arabs that Jesus, son of Mary was to return. His bases for telling the

Arabs 1400 years ago about that specific prophecy is rooted in two Quranic scriptural verses:

(A) Chapter 4, verse 157: reads, *"And [for] their saying, "Indeed, we have killed the Messiah, Jesus, the son of Mary, the messenger of Allah ." And they did not kill him, nor did they crucify him; but [another] was made to resemble him to them. And indeed, those who differ over it are in doubt about it. They have no knowledge of it except the following of assumption. And they did not kill him, for certain."*

And,

(B) chapter 3:55: *(It was part of His countering their scheme) when God said: "Jesus, (as your mission has ended,) I will take you back (to Myself) and raise you up to Myself, and will purify you of (the groundless slanders of) those who disbelieve, and set your followers above those who disbelieve until the Day of Resurrection. Then, to Me you will all return, and I will judge between you concerning all that on which you were used to differ."*

The meaning behind these two Quranic verses were referring to a future Jesus who returns after escaping a death plot under Allah's plan. Therefore, Prophet Muhammad interpreted these meaningful verses and words to his followers over 1,400 years ago. He said:

"By Him in whose hands my soul is, the son of Mary (Jesus) will shortly descend amongst you people (Muslims) as a just ruler and will break the cross and kill

the pig and abolish the jizya (a tax taken from the non-Muslims, who are in the protection, of the Muslim government). Then there will be abundance of money and no-body will accept charitable gifts.[37]"

This prophetic interpretation spoken by Prophet Muhammad to his followers 1,400 years ago, represented the role of a future man to fulfill during the last days we now live. Don't expect the common Arab speaker to tell you how the prophecy is being fulfilled today. He or she does not comprehend beyond what occurred, religiously, 1,400 years ago.

In terms of what we call, the Christian version of Prophet Muhammad's words about Jesus, the Christian's have it written in their book of Gospels and Revelation too. For example, in the book of the Gospels (Luke 2:1-7), we read that a women named Mary gave birth to Jesus during the rule of Caesar Augustus.

*"Caesar Augustus (23 September 63 BC – **19 August AD** 14) was **the first Roman emperor, reigning from 27 BC** until his death in AD 14. His status as the founder of the Roman Principate (the first phase of the Roman Empire) has consolidated an enduring legacy as one of the most effective and controversial leaders in human history. The*

---

[37] Narrated Abu Huraira, Allah's Apostle said, (Bukhari Volume 3, Book 34, Number 425)

reign of Augustus initiated an era of relative peace known as the Pax Romana. "[38]

After the rule of Caesar Augustus, Tiberius Caesar Augustus took ruler ship over Rome.

[Tiberius] reigning from AD 14 to 37. *He succeeded his stepfather, Augustus. Tiberius was one of Rome's greatest generals.*[39]

At that juncture, after Jesus was born, the Christians say he was crucified and died April 3, 33 AD. But, actually he escaped death only to be exalted into the presence of God to take a sealed book. (See Revelations 5:5-6) Be mindful, all of the previous biblical story had already taken place during gospel era of his life up to 33 AD. Then in Revelation 12:5, it reveals the history about another women named Mary giving birth to a child whose future was to rule the nations with an Iron rod – justice.

If you continue reading the book of Revelations (66th and final book of Bible), you realize both, the Jesus of the Gospel and the male child of revelations were taken or exalted. Of the two servants of God, one returns to rule the nations of the earth after receiving a piece of a new sealed book. (See Revelations 10).

---

[38] Augustus - Wikipedia

[39] Tiberius - Wikipedia

People around the planet are so thankful for the life of Jesus (Isa) and his mother Mary (Maryam) of 2000 years ago. Both lived during the time of Caesar Augustus and Tiberius of Rome. It is clear, however, her son was so hated by the government of Roman that Rome did not retain neither he nor his mother's life actual life into official public records. But Rome recorded the history of Spartacus and his slave revolt. Why?

Sadly, by the time the history of Jesus' life was written in 70 C.E., his honorable life in Palestine/Jerusalem had been misinterpreted by the Jews and mythicized into religiosity.

But today, the myth is removed and the sign of Jesus and his mother is being fulfilled in Black America!

"And We made the son of Mary and his mother as a Sign: We gave them both shelter on high ground, affording rest and security and furnished with springs." Holy Quran 23:50

Another honoring verse about Jesus (Isa) and his mother Mary (Maryam) said:

"And (remember) her who guarded her chastity: We breathed into her of Our spirit, and We made her and her son a sign for all peoples." Holy Quran 21:91

Prophet Muhammad said he saw two divine men returning. One name Mahdi and the other named Jesus.

"The Mahdi (Arabic: ٱلْمَهْدِيّ, al-mahdīy), meaning "the Rightly Guided One", is an eschatological Messianic figure who, according to Islamic belief, will appear at the end of times to rid the world of evil and injustice. In Muslim traditions, it is said that he will appear alongside Jesus Christ and establish the Divine kingdom of God." [40]

Don't expect the common English speaker to tell you how the prophecy is being fulfilled today. He or she does not comprehend beyond what the white man could not tell you nor any Islamic scholar. For they are also stuck in their medieval interpretations.

Your answers to the divine historical secrets hiding the life, so-called death and mission of the prophetic "JESUS" can be comprehended by studying the history of two men. The Honorable Elijah Muhammad, spiritually born in 1931, and his helper, The Honorable Minister Louis Farrakhan, spiritually born in 1955. Thus the reason why Jesus whom Luke sees and the male child whom Revelation sees a birth 24 chapters apart. And so to, were Elijah Muhammad and Minister Farrakhan spiritual birth 24 years apart. Simply put, the 24 chapters from Luke to Revelation and the 24 years from 1931 (year Elijah met Master Fard Muhammad) and 1955 (year Louis met Honorable Elijah Muhammad) fulfilled the mathematical theology revealing what Satan tried to hide by changing the original words of scripture.

---

[40] "Hadith – Chapters on Al-Fitan – Jami' at-Tirmidhi – Sunnah.com – Sayings and Teachings of Prophet Muhammad

We shall conclude this little book, by identifying the woman who gave physical birth to Elijah Poole (Muhammad) and the woman who gave physical birth to Louis Walcott (Farrakhan).

The first man, Elijah Muhammad's mother (exhibit a) was named **Mariah**--a variant of the name **Maria**—Latinized is **Mary**. And of course, the second man, Minister Farrakhan's mother (exhibit b) whom is unveiled by her name **Mae**, nick name for **Mary**.

Exhibit a)   Exhibit b)

Appendix I Master Fard Muhammad

Wallace D. Muhammad (Imam W. Deen Mohammed) was not the first to misrepresent the person of Master Fard Muhammad, the Teacher of his father.

On Wednesday November 30, 1932 the Detroit Free Press released a report from the authorities of the mental hospital after holding Master Fard Muhammad et al five days. The report, in part, read:

"...Indications are that Robert Harris, slayer of Smith, is mentally unbalanced, doctors reported, although an official diagnosis of his case will not be made until a specially appointed sanity commission reports its findings to Recorder's Court Judge John P. Scallen on Dec. 6."

"Wallace Farad, confessed 'Arabian' founder of the cult, apparently was not driven to his sinister teachings through insanity, the report states."

"However, all of the men are being kept in the psychopathic ward of the hospital pending further investigation."[41]

Notice what words were used concerning "Wallace Farad" and his state of mind. Then consider the following Biblical verse as it relates fully to what happened in 1932 with respect to

---

[41] http://mythicdetroit.org/index.php?n=Main.VoodooMurdersCoverage#toc1

the three year ministry of The True Masters arrest and detainment?

"You brought me this man as one who was misleading the people. When I examined him before you, I did not find this man guilty of anything you accused him of doing." (Luke 23:14)

Photo of Master W. Fard Muhammad reading the Holy Quran

Read carefully what Master Fard Muhammad told the detective who arrested him in 1932.

"...Farad [Fard] was taken into custody Wednesday morning as he was leaving his room in a hotel at 1 W. Jefferson Ave. He did not resist the officers, smiling enigmatically when told he was under arrest...At Police Headquarters he evaded questions cleverly."

*"With the complacent smile of the Oriental fakir, Farad calmly told detectives the he was the **"supreme being on earth**...'* [42]

Take note! The finder of the members of the Lost and Found Nation of Islam told the arresting officer, "*I am the supreme being on earth*". This was on November 24, 1932. He further said:

"Islamism, he proudly declared, has large followings in cities throughout the country, among which are Chicago, New York, and Philadelphia. Members frequently visit other chapters in different cities, he said." [43]

Hopefully you can comprehend why Master Fard Muhammad is the first of two other men whom he prepared to uphold "His Nation" *The Nation of Islam*. Much more history is to unfold. Divine prophecy will not be defeated. God in Person indeed has visited America! Not Palestine or Jerusalem.2000 years ago, but North America.

---

[42] http://mythicdetroit.org/index.php?n=Main.VoodooMurdersCoverage#toc1

[43] ibid

Appendix ii, Ethiopian Bible

Ethiopian Bible is the oldest and complete bible on earth. Written in Ge'ez an ancient language of Ethiopia it's nearly 800 years older than the King James Version and contains 81-88 books compared to 66. It includes the Book of ENOCH, Esdras, Buruch and all 3 Books of MACCABEE, and a host of others that was excommunicated from the KJV.

To bring clarity to the above information, you must comprehend what Elijah Muhammad wrote on August 18, 1934 in "The Final Call to Islam" newspaper he published as Elijah Muhammad, Minister of Islam in North America. The article entitled was entitled, *"Bible Nothing But Warning Book to Black Man of America"*. It reads:

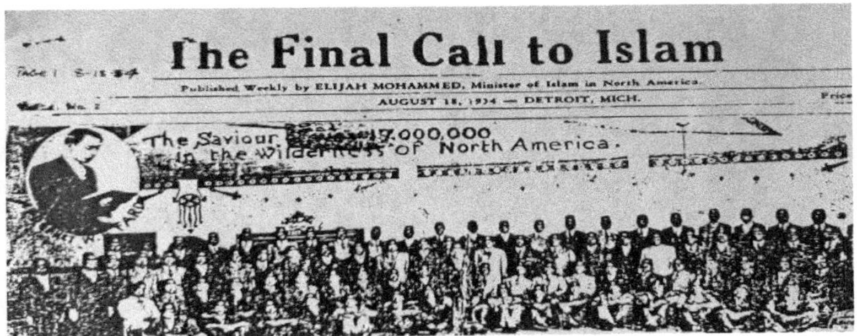

"The who's contents of the Bible that you have, predict the return of us back to Islam and Asia, our home. But remember that the same devils who enslaved our forfathers and ourselves DILUTED THE TRUTH IN THE BIBLE when they translated it out of the Greek tongues into English language. It was originally given to the Hebrews by the Ethiopians (Moslems). The Asiatic Moslems knew that they would have a lost brother somewhere on the Planet Earth. But the Holy Quran did not say where he would be. But they all believed that in the devils's civilization was where their lost brother would be. So they gave this warning Book (Bible) to the Jews (devils) that perchance if the lost brother would see its contents he would rise from the death of ignorance to the call of the Messenger....(Malachi 4:5)"

Recommended Book to Read